30minute SEDER™

www.30minuteseder.com

THE HAGGADAH THAT BLENDS BREVITY WITH TRADITION

" Rabbinically Approved... ★★★★
This meaningful abbreviated format includes all of the highlights of the traditional Seder. The gender sensitive, socially conscious text will appeal to all ages."

Rabbi Bonnie Koppell

" It's user friendly...it will appeal to just about every branch of Judaism." Menachem Youlus - owner of the Jewish Book Store of Greater Wash.

Washington Post

" Your Haggadah saved my Seder! It was so nice not to hear complaints of "when do we eat?" from guests. 30minute-Seder will be on our Passover table for many years to come."

Sally Cohen

See our unique Passover items at: www.30minuteSeder.com

Published by: 30minute-Seder, LLC   Scottsdale, AZ 85254
Printed in USA. ISBN 978-0-9791256-0-7

Please address all inquiries to: info@30minuteSeder.com

Passc

All the elements of an exciting story...
slavery and oppression followed by freedom and redemption

...with hope for the future.

That's probably why many people name Passover as their favorite Jewish holiday. And while this Haggadah is designed to educate us about our past, it is also written to help us appreciate what we have today. It encourages dialogue with our children by asking questions, giving examples and telling stories. It takes us from the time when we were slaves and had to eat the bread of affliction – through the time we were freed and chose to eat Matzah, the bread of freedom.

ver...

It's a story that has a sad beginning
...and a happy ending.

The Seder

is a time to reflect on those less fortunate than ourselves, as well as the good fortune we now enjoy. In that spirit, let no stranger be alone on Seder night and invite anyone who wishes to participate. We were once all slaves to Pharaoh and...

we were freed by the mighty hand of God.

Preparation for the Seder

Chametz Removal

Before the sun sets and we sit down for our Seder, it is customary—as well as commanded by the Torah—to remove all "chametz" from the home. "Chametz" is any food that's been leavened, especially the five grains of wheat, barley, spelt, rye, and oats. Matzah is unleavened bread, so it's okay!

One tradition carried over from Eastern Europe has a member of the household hide ten pieces of bread around the house, followed by an after dark search on the night before Passover. The head of the household, by flashlight or candlelight, searches each room for hidden chametz. Once the bread is found, a feather is used to sweep any stray crumbs onto a wooden spoon, which is then all burned together.

This removal of chametz is preceded by the following prayer:

Blessed are You, Adonai our God, Creator of the universe, Who makes us holy with Your mitzvot, and Who commanded us concerning the removal of Chametz.

To symbolize the search and removal of all chametz at the Seder, each person should look under their plate and remove (or pretend to remove) any traces of chametz they may find there.

Immediately following the search, the following prayer is said:

Any chametz, which is in my possession that I did or did not see, which I did or did not remove, shall be nullified and be ownerless as the dust of the earth.

Holiday / Sabbath Candle Lighting

Each table should have festival or Sabbath candles to be lit for Passover. If Passover falls on a Friday night, add the prayer words (in parentheses).

Blessed are You, Adonai our God, Creator of the universe, Who makes us holy with your mitzvot, who commanded us to light (Sabbath and) festival candles.

Blessed are You, Adonai our God, Creator of the universe, Who gave us life, sustained us, and enabled us to reach this season of joy.

The Seder

Opening Prayer

May all who are enslaved throughout the world, come to know freedom. May all who are free, appreciate the blessings of abundance. And may all of us dwell in the house of God and give thanks for our good fortune as we celebrate these rituals of Passover.

The Seder Plate

The Seder plate contains the main symbols that help us tell the story of Passover.

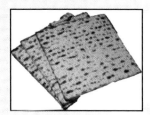

Matzah — There are 3 whole matzot placed one on top of the other, separated and covered by a cloth or napkin. Many matzah covers are available for purchase, and in some homes, the children make the covers. Since you'll be eating matzah many times throughout the Seder, make sure that there's enough for everyone to have an adequate portion.

Maror and Chazeret — These are the bitter herbs symbolizing the bitter life the Jews led while they were slaves in Egypt, which are eaten twice during the Seder, once by themselves and another time with matzah. You can use several different vegetables that qualify as maror, two of which are put on your Seder plate in the spaces marked maror and chazeret. Red or white horseradish is often used for maror and romaine lettuce for chazeret.

Charoset — Charoset should be made to look like mortar because it is symbolic of the bricks and mortar the slaves used in making the Egyptian buildings. One traditional recipe calls for a mixture of grated apples, nuts, and cinnamon mixed with a little red wine.

Zeroa — A roasted bone (often a lamb shank or chicken bone) is placed on the Seder plate. The bone serves as a symbol of God's mighty arm that convinced the Egyptians to free the slaves. It also represents the Paschal lamb that was used as a special sacrifice in the days of the ancient Temple in Jerusalem.

Beitzah — A hard-boiled or roasted egg represents the second sacrifice that was offered on the eve of Passover at the Temple. The egg is quite popular as it serves as a symbol of mourning, and is used as a reminder of our sadness caused by the destruction of the Holy Temple. The round shape also reminds us of the circle of life.

Karpas — A vegetable other than bitter herbs (parsley, for example) is placed on the Seder plate. Since Passover was also an agricultural festival celebrated by our ancestors, karpas represents the arrival of spring. It will be dipped in salt water and eaten. In some traditions, a potato, onion, or other vegetable is used and is considered the "appetizer". It is also dipped in salt water and eaten.

Salt Water — This represents the sweat and tears of our ancestors in bondage. While it's not actually part of the Seder plate, a small bowl of salt water should be placed conveniently nearby. Where many people are present, several bowls should be placed around the table for the dipping of karpas.

Wine — Four cups of wine are consumed during the Seder (grape juice may be substituted for some or all of the wine). Why four? They serve as a reminder of the four references to Redemption that are mentioned in the Book of Exodus:

I will bring you out of Egypt.
I will deliver you from bondage.
I will redeem you with an outstretched arm.
I will take you to Me for a people.

It is traditional that each person's cup be filled by the person sitting next to them, to symbolize the majesty of the evening, as though each person had a servant (at least for the night). During the Seder proceedings, whenever wine is consumed, it is customary to drink the entire cup.

Blessing Over the Wine

Fill the wine cup of the person sitting next to you, then raise your cup of wine and recite the following:

בָּרוּךְ אַתָּה יְיָ, אֱלֹהֵינוּ מֶלֶךְ הָעוֹלָם, בּוֹרֵא פְּרִי הַגָּפֶן.

Baruch Atah Adonai Eloheinu melech ha'olam borei p'ri hagafen.

Blessed are You, Adonai our God, Creator of the universe, Who creates the fruit of the vine.

Blessed are You, Adonai our God, Creator of the universe, Who has chosen us from all nations, raised us above all tongues, and made us holy with Your mitzvot.

And You, Adonai our God, have lovingly given us, (Sabbaths for rest and) festivals for rejoicing, holidays and seasons for gladness, (this Sabbath day and) this Festival of Matzah, the season of our freedom, a holy gathering in remembrance of the Exodus from Egypt.

For You have chosen and made us holy above all peoples, and Your holy (Shabbat and) festivals, in joy and gladness, You granted us as a heritage.

8

Blessed are You, Adonai, Who makes holy (the Shabbat and) Israel, and the festive seasons.

Blessed are You, Adonai our God, Creator of the universe, Who has kept us alive, sustained us, and brought us to this season.

Drink the cup of wine while reclining. To exaggerate our awareness of freedom and wealth, it is customary to recline leaning to the left, as did the aristocracy in ancient times.

Washing of the Hands (Urechatz)

Everyone now washes their hands at the sink or at the table by pouring water onto their hands into a basin. If you like, the leader can wash his or her hands on behalf of everyone as a symbolic act of preparation for the Seder and the Passover feast. Since there's no meal served at this time, there is no prayer recited.

Dipping of Vegetable / Appetizer (Karpas)

Everyone takes a vegetable other than maror (usually parsley, potato, onion, or whatever is used for karpas on the Seder plate) and dips it into salt water. The following blessing is recited before the vegetable is eaten:

בָּרוּךְ אַתָּה יְיָ, אֱלֹהֵינוּ מֶלֶךְ הָעוֹלָם, בּוֹרֵא פְּרִי הָאֲדָמָה.

Baruch Atah Adonai Eloheinu melech ha'olam borei p'ri ha'adamah.

Blessed are You, Adonai our God, Creator of the universe, Who creates the fruit of the earth.

Breaking of Matzah / Creation of Afikoman (Yachatz)

The leader uncovers the matzah and breaks the middle matzah in two, places the smaller part back between the whole matzot, and wraps up the larger part in a cloth or napkin (or Afikoman bag) for later use as the Afikoman. The leader places the Afikoman portion on their shoulder and says:

"In haste did we go out of Egypt."

At this point, the children will hide the Afikoman for the leader or the head of the household to find later. An alternate version of this tradition is to have someone hide the Afikoman for the children to find later on, after the meal.

The Story of Passover (Maggid)

The broken matzah is lifted for all to see as the leader recites:

This matzah is a symbol of affliction and poverty. The story of Passover tells us about the hardships and suffering that our ancestors endured. It reminds us of those who are in need today, so we say: "whoever is hungry, come share our food–and celebrate Passover! To those who are poor or oppressed; we pray for them and hope that the coming year will bring a better life for all."

The Four Questions

Pour the second cup of wine (don't drink it yet!) and have the youngest present ask the following:

מַה נִּשְׁתַּנָּה הַלַּיְלָה הַזֶּה מִכָּל הַלֵּילוֹת?

Mah nishtanah halailah hazeh mikol haleilot?

Why is this night different from all other Nights?

The leader now asks:

In what ways do you find this night different?

The youngest makes the following statement and then gives four examples of how this night is different:

In 4 ways do I find this night different.

שֶׁבְּכָל הַלֵּילוֹת אָנוּ אוֹכְלִין חָמֵץ וּמַצָּה הַלַּיְלָה הַזֶּה כֻּלּוֹ מַצָּה.

Sheb'chol haleilot anu ochlin chameits u'matzah, halaylah hazeh kulo matzah.

On all other nights we may eat chametz and matzah, but on this night, only matzah.

שֶׁבְּכָל הַלֵּילוֹת אָנוּ אוֹכְלִין שְׁאָר יְרָקוֹת הַלַּיְלָה הַזֶּה מָרוֹר.

Sheb'chol haleilot anu ochlin sh'ar y'rakot, halaylah hazeh maror.

On all other nights we eat many vegetables, but on this night, only maror.

שֶׁבְּכָל הַלֵּילוֹת אֵין אָנוּ מַטְבִּילִין אֲפִילוּ פַּעַם אֶחָת הַלַּיְלָה הַזֶּה שְׁתֵּי פְעָמִים.

Sheb'chol haleilot ein anu matbilin afilu pa'am echat, halaylah hazeh sh'tei f'amim.

On all other nights we don't dip even once, but on this night, we dip twice.

שֶׁבְּכָל הַלֵּילוֹת אָנוּ אוֹכְלִין בֵּין יוֹשְׁבִין וּבֵין מְסֻבִּין הַלַּיְלָה הַזֶּה
כֻּלָּנוּ מְסֻבִּין.

Sh'b'chol haleilot anu ochlin bein yoshvin uvein m'subin, Halaylah hazeh kulanu m'subin.

On all other nights we eat either sitting up or reclining, but on this night, we all recline.

Answering the Questions

The four questions are, in fact, not four questions at all. They are four statements that clarify the main question of the Seder: "Why is this night different from all other nights?" This night is different from all other nights, because on this night we tell the story of Passover as inscribed in the Book of Exodus. This night is also different because we participate in rituals that have been observed at Passover Seders for centuries by our Jewish ancestors.

We remind ourselves every year at this time that we were slaves to Pharaoh in Egypt, and God took us out with a mighty hand and an outstretched arm. If God had not liberated our ancestors from Egyptian slavery, then we, and our children, and our children's children, might still be slaves in the land of Egypt. Even if we know the story well and have told it many times, it is essential to be reminded of the details so we don't forget. By recognizing the oppression of our enslaved ancestors, we gain a greater appreciation of the freedom we enjoy today.

As we participate in the rituals of the Seder, we should not only make sure the story of Passover is told, and the significance of each component of the Seder is explained, but we should also engage the children in the proceedings. The children are encouraged to ask questions regarding the rituals of the evening. If they don't, the elders take on the role of teacher and explain using language appropriate to each child's ability to understand.

The Four Children

The four children...The wise, wicked, simple, and too young to ask. Most of us have shown qualities of the four children in our lives at one time or another.

Because we all learn in different ways and at our own pace, when sharing the meaning of Passover with children, it's important to approach them in a way that best-suits their ever-evolving personalities and abilities to learn.

The Wise Child

The "wise" or studious child likes to study and analyze the details. Give this child the tools to discover the meaning of Passover on their own and explain to them why it's important to retell the story of Exodus each year.

The Wicked Child

The "wicked" or rebellious child probably wants little to do with Passover and they exclude themselves from getting involved. A typical response can be, "What's this got to do with me?" Explain that Passover is a celebration of the freedom we all enjoy. Since this child usually lacks empathy, ask questions that get them involved, like "How would it feel if you were a slave and freed by God?"

The Simple Child

For a "simple" child who is easily overwhelmed, give a simple explanation. Don't confuse them with details; instead tell them the basic facts of the story, and explain the general meaning of Passover in terms they can understand.

The Child too Young to Ask

Maybe they're too young to form a question, or unable to ask one because they simply don't understand. Perhaps this child of God may be an adult that lacks the capacity to speak, or lives with some other disability. Treat them with love, understanding, and patience, and explain the meaning of Passover in terms that they can relate to. Try telling stories or singing songs, and make it a festive time.

We Toast Our Endurance as a People

The matzot are covered and the wine cup is lifted as the following paragraph is proclaimed joyously:

Throughout the ages we have endured. For not only has one risen against us to annihilate us, but in every generation they rise against us to annihilate us. But Adonai, the Holy One of Blessing, rescues us from their hand.

Put down the wine cup and uncover the matzot.

Let My People Go!

We weren't always slaves in Egypt. We became slaves... and the story of how we became slaves to the Pharaohs of Egypt, and ultimately how we were freed, is really the basis of the story of Passover. It's a part of history that belongs to all of us. By telling this story year after year, we're ensuring that we'll never forget our oppression or our freedom.

As with most of religious history, the story has been passed on from generation to generation, and tonight, especially if there are children present, you're perpetuating an important ritual.

Many years ago, in the land of Egypt, Joseph, the son of Jacob and Rachel, was sold into slavery by his brothers. Joseph was skilled and intelligent and soon became an official in the court of the Egyptian Pharaoh.

Joseph could interpret dreams, which he sometimes used to predict the future. He offered the Pharaoh his prediction of an upcoming famine, which the Pharaoh heeded.

Because Joseph's timely advice saved the land from a great famine, Pharaoh invited them to stay when Joseph's family came to Egypt searching for food. They lived in peace for many years and became known as Israelites.

Years later, a new Pharaoh came to rule. He did not remember Joseph and all he had done for the Egyptians. He saw that the Israelites' population was growing rapidly, and feared that in a war they might side with the enemy and become a danger to Egypt.

To remove this "problem of the Israelites", Pharaoh enslaved them. He forced them to work hard, building his cities and palaces. Baking bricks and carrying stones in the desert heat, they knew neither peace nor rest, only misery and pain. To limit their population, Pharaoh decreed, "Every baby boy born to an Israelite woman shall be drowned in the river."

In an effort to save their baby, Amram and Yocheved, a Jewish slave couple, hid him in a basket on the riverbank. When Pharaoh's daughter, the princess, came down to the river to bathe, she found the baby and decided to take him home to the palace. The princess named the baby, Moses; which means, "brought out of the water."

Because she needed a nurse to feed and care for the baby, the princess looked for a Jewish nurse. Yocheved's daughter, Miriam, who was hiding by the river watching, came out and told the princess that she knew of a nurse. She ran home and brought Yocheved back to the princess, not revealing that she was really Moses' mother. Yocheved became Moses' nurse and was able to care for him throughout his childhood.

Moses, being the adopted son of the princess, would have lived a rich life in the Pharaoh's palace, but he could not bear to see his people suffer as slaves. One day, he came upon an Egyptian taskmaster who was beating an Israelite slave. In a fit of rage, Moses beat the Egyptian to death. His crime soon became known and Moses was forced to leave his homeland and flee into the desert. Wandering around the desert, he came upon a family of shepherds in the land of Midian. He was taken in and became a shepherd himself.

One day while tending to his sheep, Moses came upon a bush that was on fire. Although it was burning, it was not being consumed. He heard God's voice coming from the bush, telling Moses to go back to Egypt and free his people from slavery—and lead them out of Egypt. Because Moses was merely a shepherd, he asked God, "How may I accomplish this great task, I am but a lowly shepherd, and I am of impaired speech." God replied, "Go forth to Egypt with your wooden staff. I will be by your side and the Pharaoh will be forced to free your people."

THE 10

Moses returned to Egypt...

and went to see the Pharaoh with his brother Aaron, as his spokesperson. "*Let my people go!*" Moses demanded. But Pharaoh had a hardened heart and refused. Through Moses, God brought forth ten plagues on the people of Egypt. The plagues at first amused the Pharaoh, but soon frightened him. The Pharaoh promised to free the slaves several times, but God hardened the Pharaoh's heart many times, and each time he agreed to free the Israelite slaves, Pharaoh went back on his word.

 SONG: GO DOWN MOSES (pg.28)

After the ninth plague, God said to Moses, "I will bring one more plague upon Pharaoh and upon Egypt. Toward midnight I will go forth among the Egyptians, and every firstborn in the land of Egypt shall die, from the firstborn of Pharaoh who sits on his throne to the firstborn of the slave girl who is behind the millstones; and all the firstborn of the cattle. And there shall be a loud cry in all the land of Egypt such as has never been or will ever be again..."

God then instructed Moses to tell his people to take a lamb from among their flocks and sacrifice it at twilight; taking some of the blood to paint a mark on the two doorposts and lintel of their homes. Moses was further instructed by God to have his people roast the lamb over a fire and eat it with unleavened bread and with bitter-herbs that same night.

PLAGUES

At midnight, God brought forth the tenth and most devastating plague; the killing of the firstborn. In every Egyptian household, the firstborn child suddenly took ill and died, but the plague "passed over" the homes of the Israelite slaves. It was then that the Pharaoh finally agreed to free the Israelites.

While we celebrate the freeing of the Israelites from slavery, God has instructed us to take no pleasure in the suffering of the Egyptians. To commemorate their suffering, each person dips their little finger into their wine and places a drop on their plate as we recite the ten plagues that God brought down upon the Egyptians.

Blood דָּם
Frogs צְפַרְדֵּעַ
Lice כִּנִּים
Wild Beasts עָרוֹב
Cattle-Plague דֶּבֶר
Boils שְׁחִין
Hail בָּרָד
Locusts אַרְבֶּה
Darkness חֹשֶׁךְ
Killing of the Firstborn מַכַּת בְּכוֹרוֹת

Moses did not trust the Pharaoh...

He told his people to quickly pack whatever they could carry, and Moses led them out of Egypt into the desert. With no time to bake their bread, the people carried their kneading bowls and their dough, wrapped in cloaks upon their shoulders. Once free and in the desert, they baked the dough on the hot rocks into matzah.

But once again the Pharaoh changed his mind—and sent his soldiers to capture the Israelites. As Pharaoh's army caught up with the Israelites at the Red Sea, God told Moses to hold up his wooden staff. Suddenly, a huge wind came up and the Red Sea parted—allowing all the freed slaves to pass. Once all of the Israelites were safely across, Moses again held up his staff and the waters closed upon the Pharaoh's soldiers killing all of them.

Finally...
the Israelites were truly free!

As a way of giving praise to God, and showing appreciation for all the blessings given us, we recite Dayenu (It would have been enough and we are grateful). After each line is read, everyone present proclaims...

Dayenu !

Had God brought us out of Egypt, but not executed judgments against the Egyptians, it would have been enough.

Had God executed judgments against them, but not upon their gods, it would have been enough.

Had God executed judgments against their gods, but not slain their firstborn, it would have been enough.

Had God slain their firstborn, but not given us their wealth, it would have been enough.

Had God given us their wealth, but not split the Sea for us, it would have been enough.

Had God split the Sea for us, but not led us through it on dry land, it would have been enough.

Had God led us through it on dry land, but not drowned our oppressors in it, it would have been enough.

Had God drowned our oppressors in it, but not provided for our needs in the desert for forty years, it would have been enough.

Had God provided for our needs in the desert for forty years, but not fed us the Manna, it would have been enough.

Had God fed us the Manna, but not given us the Sabbath, it would have been enough.

Had God given us the Sabbath, but not brought us to Mount Sinai, it would have been enough.

Had God brought us to Mount Sinai, but not given us the Torah, it would have been enough.

Had God given us the Torah, but not brought us into the Land of Israel, it would have been enough.

בָּרוּךְ אַתָּה "

Thank You God, for all the favors You have bestowed upon us! You led us out of Egypt, slavery, and oppression. You brought the plagues against the Egyptians, slew their firstborn, and brought us their wealth. You split open the Red Sea, then drowned our oppressors. Thank You for taking care of us in the desert for forty years. You fed us Manna, gave us the Sabbath, then brought us to Mount Sinai to give us the Torah and Your commandments. Thank You, oh God, for bringing us to the Land of Israel, making us a great nation.

 **SONG:** DAYENU (pg.29)

30 minute SEDER

The matzot are covered; we raise the glass of wine, and recite the following together:

We join together to glorify and bless God for bringing us out of slavery and bondage; for granting us our freedom; and for turning our sorrow into joy. We give thanks to God for helping us reach this night so that we may carry out the rituals of the Seder, eating the offerings and symbolic sacrifices, while singing praise for our redemption and freedom.

בָּרוּךְ אַתָּה יְיָ, אֱלֹהֵינוּ מֶלֶךְ הָעוֹלָם, בּוֹרֵא פְּרִי הַגָּפֶן.

Baruch Atah Adonai Eloheinu melech ha'olam borei p'ri hagafen.

Blessed are You, Adonai our God, Creator of the universe, Who creates the fruit of the vine.

Drink the second cup of wine while reclining, leaning to the left side. When your cup is drained, have the person sitting next to you refill it.

The Symbols of Passover

One of Judaism's greatest scholars, Rabbi Gamliel, decreed that the Seder is not complete unless we explain the meaning of the three main symbols of Pesach, matzah, and maror.

Point to the Pesach (roasted bone) and say:

This bone represents the mighty arm of God that convinced the Egyptians to free the slaves. It also represents the Paschal lamb that was used as a special sacrifice in the days of the ancient Temple in Jerusalem.

Blessing Over Bread / Matzah (Motzi)

The leader raises all the matzot on the Seder plate and recites the following:

בָּרוּךְ אַתָּה יְיָ, אֱלֹהֵינוּ מֶלֶךְ הָעוֹלָם, הַמּוֹצִיא לֶחֶם מִן הָאָרֶץ.

Baruch Atah Adonai Eloheinu melech ha'olam hamotzi lechem min ha'aretz.

Blessed are You, Adonai our God, Creator of the universe, Who brings forth bread from the earth.

בָּרוּךְ אַתָּה יְיָ, אֱלֹהֵינוּ מֶלֶךְ הָעוֹלָם, אֲשֶׁר קִדְּשָׁנוּ בְּמִצְוֹתָיו וְצִוָּנוּ עַל אֲכִילַת מַצָּה.

Baruch Atah Adonai Eloheinu melech ha'olam asher kid'shanu b'mitzvotav v'tzivanu al achilat matzah.

Blessed are You, Adonai our God, Creator of the universe, Who makes us holy with Your commandments, and has instructed us in the eating of matzah.

Give each participant a piece from each of the top two matzot and recite the following:

We now take this matzah; for not only is it commanded in the Torah by God, "Seven days you shall eat unleavened bread...", but this matzah also symbolizes the unleavened bread our ancestors ate while in the desert, and in their great haste while fleeing Egypt. Because they did not have time to allow the dough to rise, they were forced to bake their dough before it leavened, and eat it in the form of hard, flat, crackers, which we now call matzah.

The matzah should now be eaten while reclining, leaning to the left side.

Blessing Over Bitter Herbs (Maror)

Each participant takes a small spoonful of maror and charoset. The maror symbolizes the bitter life of slavery, while charoset represents the mortar used by the slaves to build the Pharaoh's cities. Recite the following blessing, and then eat them together:

בָּרוּךְ אַתָּה יְיָ אֱלֹהֵינוּ מֶלֶךְ הָעוֹלָם, אֲשֶׁר קִדְּשָׁנוּ בְּמִצְוֹתָיו וְצִוָּנוּ עַל אֲכִילַת מָרוֹר.

Baruch Atah Adonai Eloheinu melech ha'olam asher kid'shanu b'mitzvotav v'tzivanu al achilat maror.

Blessed are You, Adonai our God, Creator of the universe, who makes us holy with Your mitzvot, and has commanded us concerning the eating of maror.

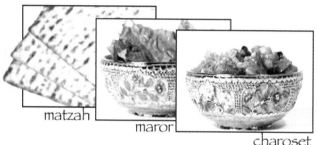

matzah

maror

charoset

Hillel's Sandwich (Korech)

It is written in the Torah: "They shall eat it [the Passover sacrifice or Paschal lamb] with matzah and bitter herbs." Rabbi Hillel, a revered scholar who lived while the Temple still stood, used to combine the Passover offerings of the Paschal lamb, matzah, and maror and eat them together in a sandwich. Since we no longer have a Paschal lamb at our Seder table, we now use matzah, maror, and charoset, to make the sandwich.

The bottom matzah is now taken and we make a sandwich of matzah, maror, and charoset. Chazeret, the second bitter herb is often used here as the maror. It is acceptable to use both bitter herbs and to use as much charoset as you like, as long as the bitter taste is present.

Eat the sandwich and then...

Hold up the third cup of wine and recite the following:

בָּרוּךְ אַתָּה יְיָ, אֱלֹהֵינוּ מֶלֶךְ הָעוֹלָם, בּוֹרֵא פְּרִי הַגָּפֶן.

Baruch Atah Adonai Eloheinu melech ha'olam borei p'ri hagafen.

Blessed are You, Adonai our God, Creator of the universe, Who creates the fruit of the vine.

Drink! When your cup is drained, have the person sitting next to you refill it. The cup of Elijah should be filled at this time.

Elijah the Prophet

The leader of the Seder holds up the Cup of Elijah and says:

Someday, the prophet Elijah will return to earth to lead the way for an age of Peace. In the spirit of Passover, as a celebration of freedom, we welcome Elijah into our home and to our Seder.

Someone opens the front door as the leader says:

Enter, Elijah the prophet, may you soon come and issue in the great Age of Peace!

 **SONG:** ELIYAHU HANAVI (pg.29)

Close the front door.

The Fourth Cup of Wine

Raise the glass of wine and recite the following:

בָּרוּךְ אַתָּה יְיָ, אֱלֹהֵינוּ מֶלֶךְ הָעוֹלָם, בּוֹרֵא פְּרִי הַגָּפֶן.

Baruch Atah Adonai Eloheinu melech ha'olam borei p'ri hagafen.

Blessed are You, Adonai our God, Creator of the universe, Who creates the fruit of the vine.

Drink the fourth cup of wine while reclining, leaning to the left side.

SONG: CHAD GADYA / WHO KNOWS ONE ?
& OTHER FAMILY FAVORITES...(pg.30)

Before the Traditional Seder Meal / Conclusion (Nirtzah)

It is traditional in many families to serve hard boiled eggs dipped in salt water at this time—as a symbol of spring and the beginning of new life. As with many of the symbols used for the Seder, the egg has another meaning. It reminds us of the Jewish midwives who showed bravery in refusing to follow the Pharaoh's demand that, "Every baby boy born to an Israelite woman shall be drowned in the river." This brave action ensured the survival of the Jewish nation.

At the conclusion of the meal, the Afikoman (which means dessert) is found by the leader of the Seder, often by "buying hints" from the children who hid it, and it is now distributed among all participants to be eaten. This dessert represents the sweetness of freedom to be enjoyed for the rest of the evening.

An alternate (modern) tradition is to have someone hide the Afikoman and have the children find it. A monetary reward is generally given. The amount is negotiable!

All Jews are invited to one day return to the promised land of Israel and celebrate Passover as our ancestors did. It is the desire and hope of many Jews to someday make that journey, and make Seder in Jerusalem. It is in that spirit that all present together say...

לְשָׁנָה הַבָּאָה בִּירוּשָׁלָיִם.

"L'Shana Ha'ba-a B'yerushalayim!"

Next Year in Jerusalem!"

And now...
the Passover feast begins!

Songs of the Seder

Download sheet-music and Hebrew versions for these and other popular Passover songs at www.30minuteSeder.com.

Go Down Moses
(Let My People Go)

When Israel was in Egypt land,
Let my people go.

Oppressed so hard they could not stand,
Let my people go.

Go down, Moses, way down in Egypt land,
Tell ol' Pharaoh, let my people go.

Thus saith the Lord, bold Moses said,
Let my people go.

If not I'll smite your people dead,
Let my people go.

Go down, Moses, way down in Egypt land,
Tell ol' Pharaoh, let my people go.

As Israel stood by the water side,
Let my people go.

By God's command it did divide,
Let my people go.

Go down, Moses, way down in Egypt land,
Tell ol' Pharaoh, let my people go.

return to page 16

Dayenu

Ilu hotsi, hotsianu,
hotsianu mimitsrayim,
hotsianu mimitsrayim,
Dayenu!

Da, dayenu! (3X)
Dayenu! Dayenu!

Ilu natan, natan lanu,
natan lanu et hatorah,
natan lanu et hatorah,
Dayenu!

Da, dayenu! (3X)
Dayenu! Dayenu!

Ilu natan, natan lanu,
natan lanu et hashabbat,
natan lanu et hashabbat,
Dayenu!

Da, dayenu! (3X)
Dayenu! Dayenu!

turn to page 22

Eliyahu Ha-Navi
(Elijah, the Prophet)

Eliyahu ha-Navi, Eliyahu ha-Tishbi, Eliyahu, Eliyahu,
Eliyahu ha-Giladi.

Bimhayrah v'yamenu, yavo aleynu, im Moshiach ben
David, im Moshiach ben David.

Elijah the Prophet, Elijah the Tishbite, Elijah, Elijah,
Elijah the Gileadite.

Speedily and in our days, come to us, with the Messiah, son of David, with the Messiah, son of David.

return to page 25

Passover never tasted this good!

Your SURVIVAL GUIDE to a delicious Passover.

Kosher - style
Passover
cooking made simple™

STARTERS | MAINS | SIDES | SWEETS | BREAKFAST

See our cookbook and unique passover items at:

WWW.30MINUTESEDER.COM

"Making Passover Fun!"

30minute-Seder™ is also available in
Braille, Large Print, & Downloadable "print-your-own" versions.